A HISTORY OF TOILET PAPER (AND OTHER POTTY TOOLS)

Written by
Sophia Gholz

Illustrated by
Xiana Teimoy

RP|KIDS
PHILADELPHIA

Running Press Kids
Hachette Book Group
1290 Avenue of the Americas, New York, NY 10104
www.runningpress.com/rpkids
@RP_Kids

Printed in China

First Edition: August 2022

Published by Running Press Kids, an imprint of Perseus Books, LLC, a subsidiary of Hachette Book Group, Inc.
The Running Press Kids name and logo is a trademark of the Hachette Book Group.

The Hachette Speakers Bureau provides a wide range of authors for speaking events.
To find out more, go to www.hachettespeakersbureau.com or call (866) 376-6591.

The publisher is not responsible for websites (or their content) that are not owned by the publisher.

Print book cover and interior design by Frances J. Soo Ping Chow.

Library of Congress Cataloging-in-Publication Data
Names: Gholz, Sophia M., author. | Teimoy, Xiana, illustrator.
Title: A history of toilet paper (and other potty tools) / written by Sophia Gholz ;
illustrated by Xiana Teimoy. Description: Philadelphia : Running Press Kids, 2022. |
Includes bibliographical references. | Audience: Ages 4-8 |
Identifiers: LCCN 2021002949 (print) | LCCN 2021002950 (ebook) | ISBN 9780762475551 (hardcover) |
ISBN 9780762475537 (ebook) | ISBN 9780762475544 (ebook) |
ISBN 9780762475568 (ebook) | ISBN 9780762475575 (ebook)
Subjects: LCSH: Toilet paper—History—Juvenile literature.
Classification: LCC HD9839.T32 H46 2022 (print) | LCC HD9839.T32 (ebook) | DDC 391.6/4—dc23
LC record available at https://lccn.loc.gov/2021002949
LC ebook record available at https://lccn.loc.gov/2021002950

ISBNs: 978-0-7624-7555-1 (hardcover), 978-0-7624-7554-4 (ebook),
978-0-7624-7556-8 (ebook), 978-0-7624-7557-5 (ebook)

APS

10 9 8 7 6 5 4 3 2 1

For Brendan, of course.
Thanks for always knowing everything, especially
how to have a good laugh.

—S. G.

To Guillermo Teimoy, my dearest brother.
For all those years when we shared toilet paper
(and other potty tools).

—X. T.

In the beginning, potty time meant the great outdoors,
with stones and seashells,

grass, moss, leaves,

and water or snow.

As civilizations advanced, so did technology.

Well, sort of.

Some folks used ceramic
or brick potties.

PARK YOUR REAR
RIGHT HERE.

Or simple pots.

But most people still used the great outdoors.

That is, if you didn't mind pottying in public
and sharing a *tersorium* (that's a bum brush) with others.

So, when did paper finally make an appearance beside toilets?
Well, almost two thousand years ago, a Chinese inventor named Cai Lun
wanted something easy to write on.

So he mixed and
mashed plant bark, rags, and
fishing nets until . . .

wait for it . . .

But this paper wasn't for potties. It was used for writing.
That meant the bum brush remained a popular choice.
Lightweight and easy to pack.

Don't forget your sword
and your stick, ancient warrior!

A thousand years later, Cai Lun's invention was finally used for more than just writing. Thousands of toilet paper sheets were packaged each year in China, mostly for the imperial family. If you were lucky, those large sheets may have even been scented.

OOOOO, LOVELY!

But the rest of the world had yet to catch on.

In England, a little more than four hundred years ago,
Sir John Harrington had a wild idea. It was weird. It was wacky.
It was . . . the first flushing toilet!

Now we're getting somewhere.

Queen Elizabeth fancied the futuristic flusher.
Unfortunately, it used too much water, so Harrington's invention
went bottoms up—forgotten in a flush.

About a hundred years later, in 1700s France, a contraption called the bidet brought a refreshing twist to cleanliness (albeit, a little ticklish).

Who needs paper when you can spritz?

Meanwhile, across the globe in colonial America,
outhouses and corn were a common combination.

With the rise of magazines and newspapers in the late 1800s,
a new sort of toilet paper arrived.

In fact, the *Farmer's Almanac*, a popular magazine at the time,
was made with a hole near the spine so you could hang it
in the outhouse right next to your potty.

It wasn't until 1857 that Joseph Gayetty, an inventor in New York City, introduced the first commercial toilet paper. But Gayetty's flat sheets were expensive and only advertised for medical use.

As a result, the invention went plop with the public.
Drip. Drop. Down the drain.

In 1871, another New York inventor named Seth Wheeler came up with a crafty concept when he perforated wrapping paper and rolled it up! While the invention was first meant for his wrapping paper company, he thought it might be a hit in the bathroom. And he was right!

But it was two brothers, Clarence and E. Irvin Scott, who took the paper to the potty around 1890. The Scott Brothers supplied the rolls to stores and merchants who then sold the paper to everyone.

The invention made a splash and has stuck around ever since.

Can you believe humans were around for more than 195,000 years
before they invented something as simple as toilet paper?
And now it's used for all sorts of things.

Poo . . . plant . . . and play!

Today, potty time across the globe is still as different as it was in the beginning of humankind.
But one thing is certain: whether you prefer your potty to be fancy, simple, shared,
private, or in the great outdoors—or whether you have paper, grass, sticks,
or water—when it's time to go, it's time to go.

Timeline

200,000 YEARS AGO: First *Homo sapiens* walk the earth

4TH CENTURY B.C.E. (ALMOST 2,500 YEARS AGO): Some Ancient Mesopotamians used ceramic or brick non-flushing toilets

79 A.D. (ABOUT 1,940 YEARS AGO): Ancient Romans used communal (shared) toilets with *tersorium* brushes

105 A.D. (ABOUT 1,915 YEARS AGO): Cai Lun invented paper in China during the Han Dynasty

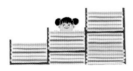

1300s: Chinese were producing thousands of paper sheets per year

1596: Sir John Harrington invents and installs a flushing toilet for Queen Elizabeth I in her palace in England

 **1600–1700s:** Outhouses were widely used in colonial America (along with corn cobs)

 **1700s:** The bidet is introduced in France

 **1800s:** Corn cobs were (mostly) swapped for newspapers and magazines in America

 **1857:** Joseph Gayetty develops commercial toilet paper and advertises it for medical use

 **1871:** Seth Wheeler receives a U.S. patent for perforated rolled wrapping paper (he later re-patents a new version for toilet paper in 1891)

 **1890:** The Scott brothers mass produce and popularize rolled toilet paper

Author's Note

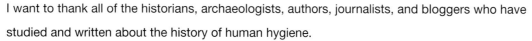

I want to thank all of the historians, archaeologists, authors, journalists, and bloggers who have studied and written about the history of human hygiene.

People, as a whole, are an inventive bunch. While researching this book, I came across a few conflicting reports about which civilization used toilet paper and flushing toilets first. Archaeologists have found evidence of flushing toilets from as early as 4,000 years ago in the Mediterranean. However, technology and developments have been forgotten and modified over the centuries. It is widely accepted that Sir John Harrington's invention in 1596 is the first modern flushing toilet. Harrington's invention, however, required twenty gallons of water, and indoor plumbing wasn't common. As a result, Harrington's potty didn't catch on at the time. It wasn't until the 1800s when Thomas Crapper reintroduced the flushing toilet that the public finally took note.

As for toilet paper, throughout history civilizations have developed and adapted different potty tools. Before Cai Lun invented his paper in China, ancient Egyptians may have used papyrus to wipe. While it is recorded that China wasn't mass producing toilet paper until the 1300s, there are historical mentions of toilet paper used in China as early as 589 A.D. Still, in those early years, wiping with papyrus, paper, or cloth would likely have been rare, an occurrence only found in certain homes.

Although Seth Wheeler and the Scott brothers are largely known for inventing and popularizing modern toilet paper as we know it, many contributed to the idea along the way.

A Glossary of Potties

ANCIENT ROMAN BATH HOUSE: These were often communal spaces with multiple toilets in the same room. In some cases, water or a small stream would run underneath the toilets to empty the waste. In ancient Roman bathrooms, a tersorium brush was used to clean your rear after using the toilet. The brush was often made of a stick of wood with a natural sponge attached to the top. When done, the brush was usually rinsed or placed into a bucket of water or vinegar until the next person was ready to use it.

BIDET: A bidet is like a sink for your rear. A bidet features a pot that you squat or sit over, while a spray of water rinses your bottom. There are different reports about who exactly invented the bidet, but it is mostly accepted that a French furniture company developed the bidet in the late 1700s.

CHAMBER POT: Chamber pots have been used for centuries. Humans have kept chamber pots in bedrooms, offices, kitchens, and more. Before indoor plumbing, chamber pots were often emptied right out the window and onto the street. Some ancient Romans, however, put their chamber pots to good use. Large pots of pee were collected around the city and taken to the public laundromat where some would wash their clothes in human pee. Urine is high in a chemical called ammonia, which is actually a natural detergent.

FLUSHING TOILET: A flushing toilet is cleaned by turning a handle or knob, often resulting in water rushing through it. There have been many versions of the flushing toilet over the centuries: some with levers, others with pulleys, and most with different plumbing plans. Some advanced cultures appear to have had versions of flushing toilets as early as 4,000 years ago. But it is recorded that Sir John Harrington invented the first modern flushing toilet in 1596.

MESOPOTAMIAN CERAMIC AND BRICK POTTIES: These were pits dug into the ground. Some included stacked ceramic cylinders or bricks on top. People would then sit or squat over the hole.

OUTHOUSE: An outhouse was a small building (usually three or four feet wide) that covered a toilet and was separate from a main building. The toilets in colonial outhouses weren't fancy. They often consisted of a hole in the ground with a wood seat overtop.

Select Bibliography

"A Mercifully Brief History of Toilet Paper." (January 24, 2018). Retrieved from History In Orbit: https://historyinorbit.com/a-mercifully-brief-history-of-toilet-paper

Alex, B. "What the Earliest Toilets Say About How Human Civilization Has Evolved." (January 31, 2020). Retrieved from Discover: https://www.discovermagazine.com/planet-earth/what-the-earliest-toilets-say-about-how-human-civilization-has-evolved

"Cai Lun." (n.d.). Retrieved from *Britannica*: https://www.britannica.com/biography/Cai-Lun

Castelow, E. "The Throne of Sir John Harrington." (n.d.). Retrieved from Historic UK: https://www.historic-uk.com/CultureUK/The-Throne-of-Sir-John-Harrington/

"History of the Bidet." (n.d.). Retrieved from Toilet Paper History: http://www.toiletpaperhistory.net/toilet-paper-history/history-of-bidet/

"Homo sapiens." (January 10, 2020). Retrieved from Smithsonian: Human Origins: http://humanorigins.si.edu/evidence/human-fossils/species/homo-sapiens

McMahon, A. (April 2016). "Trash and Toilets of Mesopotamia: Sanitation and Early Urbanism." Retrieved from The American Schools of Oriental Research (ASOR): http://www.asor.org/anetoday/2016/04/trash-and-toilets-in-mesopotamia-sanitation-and-early-urbanism/

Nash, S. E. (April 3, 2018). *What Did Ancient Romans Do Without Toilet Paper?* Retrieved from *Sapiens*: https://www.sapiens.org/column/curiosities/ancient-roman-bathrooms/

Philippe Charlier, L. B.-C. (December 17, 2012). *Toilet hygiene in the classical era.* Retrieved from *BMJ*: https://www.bmj.com/content/bmj/345/bmj.e8287.full.pdf

Ponti, C. (April 15, 2020). *All the Ways We've Wiped: The History of Toilet Paper and What Came Before.* Retrieved from History: https://www.history.com/news/toilet-paper-hygiene-ancient-rome-china

"The Hole in the Farmers' Almanac." (n.d.). Retrieved from Farmers' Almanac: https://www.farmersalmanac.com/the-hole

Wald, C. (May 24, 2016). *The secret history of ancient toilets*. Retrieved from Nature: https://www.nature.com/news/the-secret-history-of-ancient-toilets-1.19960